SPECK OF MEANING

A GUIDE TO PERSONAL GROWTH AND PURPOSE

DR. PRINCE JOSEPH

The real story behind this book — the part that's not told in its pages — is that it began as a series of conversations, messages, and late-night thoughts, advice, and guidance I shared with my daughter while she was going through the intense pressure of CBSE Grades 11 and 12. It wasn't easy to sit her down for long heart-to-heart talks, so I did what I could: I messaged her — constantly — trying to keep her encouraged, focused, and moving forward, even when things were rough.

Now she's at university, and as the dust settled, I realized that all the pain, pressure, suffering, and perseverance had left behind something — a trace of wisdom, a few lessons, and a lot of emotion.

Coincidentally, I was traveling more. Time found me — and I felt compelled to pen it all down, to give it some form.

One day, I looked at the scattered notes and thoughts and realized — the message had somehow come full circle.

Contents

Foreword — *vii*

Preface — *ix*

Acknowledgements — *xi*

Prologue — *xiii*

1. Introduction — 1

2. Good Manners – The Foundation Of Respect — 4

3. Kindness – The Strength Of A Gentle Heart — 9

4. Respect – The Foundation Of Honor And Integrity — 14

5. Responsibility – The Foundation Of Leadership, Trust, And Value — 19

6. Encouragement – Fuel For The Journey — 24

7. Discipline – The Foundation Of Growth And Leadership — 28

8. Resilience – Built To Last — 33

9. Perseverance – The Power Of Pushing Forward — 39

10. Gratitude – The Art Of Appreciating Life — 44

11. Financial Awareness – Mastering Money In A World Of Distractions — 49

12. Healthy Habits – Building A Strong Foundation For Life In The Digital Age — 56

13. Success – A Life Rich In Experience — 62

14. Applying These Lessons – Turning Knowledge Into Action — 67

15. What To Avoid – A Warning Bell For Life's Hidden — 73

Contents

Traps

16. Biases, Social Evils, And The Drug Epidemic – The   80
Hidden Chains Of Society

17. You Always Have Help – The Path Back Is Always   87
Open

18. Final Words: The Journey Ahead – Your Life, Your   95
Choices

Lets now BEGIN !   103

Foreword

This book was never meant to be a book.

It began as messages—raw, hurried, sometimes late at night—sent to my daughter while she was navigating the intense, unrelenting pressure of Grades 11 and 12 under the CBSE curriculum. Like many parents, I wanted to be there for her, not just physically, but emotionally and mentally. Yet, long conversations were hard to come by, especially with the weight of exams and expectations pressing down. So, I did the only thing I could—I typed. Words of encouragement. Reminders to pause and breathe. Thoughts on failure, discipline, kindness, and what really matters in life.

Some messages were long, some just a sentence. Some went unread in the moment, but I kept sending them anyway. Because I believed that even if a few words found their way into her heart, they might be enough to carry her through.

Now, with time passed and life moved forward—she's in university, learning and living with new energy—I find myself looking back. I realized those small exchanges had carried more meaning than I first saw. They had depth. They held lessons, not just for her, but for anyone trying to make sense of this world and their place in it.

Speck of Meaning is the form those messages took when I finally allowed myself to sit still and write them out. It's not just advice for students or young people. It's a collection of reflections—for anyone standing at the intersection of ambition and anxiety, of potential and pressure.

This isn't a perfect guidebook. But it is honest. It is drawn from real experiences—mine, my daughter's, and those I've observed closely over the years. Each chapter comes from a place of care, with the hope that it lands gently, yet firmly, in the hearts of those who read it.

If you're a parent, a student, a teacher, or simply someone trying to live a meaningful life—I hope these pages remind you that even in the chaos, a speck of meaning can make all the difference.

— Prince Joseph

Son, Brother, Friend, Peer, Chief Information Officer, Mentor, and also Father

Preface

In a world that moves fast, where expectations are high and time often feels short, we sometimes forget to pause and reflect. Speck of Meaning was born from one such pause—a moment of stillness after a long stretch of pressure, perseverance, and growth.

This book is not about perfection. It's not a manual with all the answers. Instead, it is a collection of thoughts, lessons, and values—drawn from lived experiences, pain and suffering, observations, and quiet moments of realization. These pages carry the essence of what I have shared with my daughter and what life, in turn, has shared with me.

The chapters are simple by design. Each one touches on a principle I believe is worth holding on to—kindness, resilience, respect, responsibility, gratitude, and more. These aren't just abstract ideals; they are tools to navigate real-life challenges, relationships, failures, and victories. I've tried to make them practical, heartfelt, and easy to return to when needed.

You don't have to read this book cover to cover. You can jump to any chapter that speaks to your current season. Whether you're a young adult finding your way, a parent guiding your child, or a professional recalibrating your purpose, I hope this book offers a moment of clarity, comfort, or encouragement.

If even one sentence in this book helps someone take a deep breath, see their life with a little more meaning, or make a wiser choice—then it has served its purpose.

This is my humble offering, a speck in the larger mosaic of life.

Acknowledgements

This book would not exist without the people who have shaped my life, held me up through its many seasons, and inspired the values and reflections within these pages. First and foremost, I want to thank my family—the foundation of everything I am and all I strive to be.

To the superwomen in my life: **My wife , Jitha**, whose strength, patience, and grace have been my anchor; **My mother, Mrs Leelamma**, whose unwavering faith and quiet resilience have taught me more than any book ever could;

My sisters, Ruby and Reeja, who have been constant sources of support, insight, and laughter;

and **my daughters, Judith and Rowena**, the very reason this book came to life—your journey, your courage, and your questions gave birth to these words. You each represent strength, wisdom, and unconditional love, and I am deeply grateful to walk this life with you.

To **my father, Mr Joseph**, whose presence and values continue to guide me in ways I only truly began to appreciate over time —thank you for being a quiet example of hard work, effort, consistency and perseverance.

To my peers and colleagues, past and present—you have challenged me, inspired me, and reminded me that leadership is as much about listening and learning as it is about guiding.

Many of the ideas in this book were formed through conversations, observations, and shared experiences with you.

A special word of thanks to **Mark Tharakan**, who played a big rolea big role in nudging me to take this step—your push made a quiet idea take flight.

To **Sangeeth Mohan** (ITLC)—Mr. Positive himself—thank you for being a consistent source of optimism and energy.

To **Robin Joy** (CIO, V-Guard)—I've followed your journey for years and admired the clarity and leadership you embody. Your example has been a quiet, powerful influence.

To **V.V. Jacob** (Manorama)—your recent, prolific reflective writing has been both inspiring and encouraging. You've helped me keep the momentum alive.

To the ever-enthusiastic and encouraging circle of friends at '**ISB gang and my Sanctuary**', thank you for your love, warmth, and camaraderie.

To my **NSSCE friends**—your "false negative push" (you know who you are) provided just the right blend of sarcasm and skepticism that kept me on my toes and determined to follow through. Sometimes, reverse psychology is the best kind of fuel.

To the many people who've crossed paths with me—friends, mentors, students, fellow travelers on the journey of life—thank you. You've helped shape the lens through which I see the world, and some of your stories and lessons live between the lines of this book.

And finally, I thank time itself—for the moments of reflection it offered, the quiet in-between spaces where thoughts gathered, and the unexpected windows in life's busyness that allowed me to pause and write.

Speck of Meaning is a humble offering. It carries traces of everyone mentioned here and many more unnamed. Thank you for being part of the journey.

PROLOGUE

Every journey begins quietly.

Not with grand announcements or fireworks, but with a whisper—a small thought, a simple question, or an instinctive act of care. That's how this journey began for me. Not as a writer setting out to write a book, but as a father trying to keep his daughter afloat during one of the most challenging academic phases of her life.

There were no long lectures, no speeches. Just small, consistent messages—sent between classes, late at night, after tough days. Messages that said: You've got this. Take a breath. Stay grounded. Here's what matters. I didn't realize it then, but I was writing this book one line at a time, one thought at a time.

Those moments became this manuscript. And what was once meant for one heart has found its way into a form that I now share with many.

Speck of Meaning is not a memoir. It's not a guidebook either. It's a quiet companion—something you can carry with you through the highs and lows, through confusion, doubt, excitement, and fear. Each chapter is rooted in reflection, yet aims to be refreshingly practical. Because life is not a neatly structured curriculum—it's messy, beautiful, unpredictable, and deeply personal.

This book is for those standing at crossroads, for those who've faced pressure, for those who've made mistakes and got back up, and for those who simply want to live with more clarity and kindness. It's also for the parents, teachers, mentors, and friends trying to help someone find their way.

You won't find magic formulas here. But you may find words that feel like a pause in the noise. And sometimes, that pause is all we need to rediscover what truly matters.

Every chapter is a speck. Small, but not insignificant. Together, they form something bigger—something meaningful.

This is the journey I've walked. Now I offer it to you.

I
Introduction

Introduction: Why This Book?

"Your life is your story. Make it a story worth telling."

Life doesn't come with an instruction manual, but it does leave behind clues. Throughout history, the most successful, fulfilled, and respected people—whether in leadership, business, sports, or personal life—have followed certain values, habits, and principles that helped them navigate challenges and shape their destiny.

In today's world, young people face immense pressure—from family, society, social media, and even their own expectations. There's pressure to succeed quickly, to look perfect, to make the right choices, and to stand out in a highly competitive world. But the truth is, no one has it all figured out. Even the most accomplished people started somewhere, learned through mistakes, and built their success step by step.

This book is a navigation guide—a collection of timeless principles that will help you build a strong foundation in life. It won't give you shortcuts, nor does it promise overnight success. Instead, it will equip you with the right mindset, habits, and decision-making skills to shape a future that is meaningful and fulfilling.

You might be wondering, "Why should I listen to this?" Because these principles are not just theories; they are proven by real people, past and present, who have applied them to achieve greatness. Consider this:

Abraham Lincoln was born into poverty, lost multiple elections, and failed in business before becoming one of history's greatest leaders. He didn't have a roadmap, but he had resilience, a strong work ethic, and a sense of responsibility.

Elon Musk was on the verge of financial collapse when Tesla and SpaceX nearly failed. He had no guarantees, only conviction and discipline. Today, he's one of the most influential innovators.

Serena Williams faced racism, injuries, and personal struggles but remained focused and determined, becoming one of the greatest athletes of all time.

What do these people have in common? They built their success on principles, not luck.

Through this book, you will discover the values that truly matter—discipline, respect, perseverance, integrity, responsibility, and resilience. You will learn how to apply them in education, career, business, relationships, and even in difficult moments of life.

But it's not just about what to do—it's also about what to avoid. There are pitfalls that can hold you back: procrastination, negative influences, short-term thinking, fear of failure, and self-doubt. This book will help you recognize and overcome these challenges.

Finally, remember this: Help is always available. Whether through family, mentors, faith, institutions, or guidance from books and experiences, you are never truly alone.

By the time you finish this book, you will have a clearer vision of the life you want to build, the habits that will take you there, and the mindset that will help you thrive.

Your journey starts now. Let's begin.

II

Good Manners – The Foundation of Respect

"Manners are a sensitive awareness of the feelings of others. If you have that awareness, you have good manners." – Emily Post

Why Good Manners Matter

In an increasingly digital and fast-paced world, good manners might seem like an old-fashioned idea. But they are more powerful than ever. Good manners define how we interact with others, how we are perceived, and even how far we go in life. They are not just about politeness; they are about respect, empathy, and social intelligence.

Think about the people you admire—leaders, mentors, or even friends. What makes them respected? Often, it's not just their achievements but how they treat others. Someone with good manners stands out because they show consideration, listen attentively, and create a positive atmosphere wherever they go.

Good manners open doors—whether in personal relationships, professional success, or leadership. They help in networking, career growth, and even handling conflicts with grace. Without them, even the most talented individuals struggle to earn trust and respect.

Real-Life Examples

Abraham Lincoln: Leading with Humility

Despite being the President of the United States during one of the most turbulent periods in history, Abraham Lincoln remained humble and respectful toward everyone, regardless of their social status. He would personally greet visitors to the White House and took time to write letters filled with kindness, even to political rivals. His ability to treat people with dignity and grace contributed to his legacy as one of the greatest leaders of all time.

Roger Federer: The Gentleman of Tennis

Roger Federer, one of the greatest tennis players in history, is known not just for his skill but for his grace, sportsmanship, and respect toward opponents, fans, and tournament staff. Even in defeat, he congratulates his rivals with sincerity. His reputation as a class act has earned him admiration beyond his game, proving that manners and character are just as important as talent.

These examples show that good manners are not just about etiquette; they shape your reputation and legacy.

Key Lessons from Good Manners

1. First impressions matter – People judge you in seconds, and good manners help create a strong positive impression.

1. Respect is earned, not demanded – How you treat people determines the respect you receive.

3. Kindness is a strength, not a weakness – Being polite and considerate does not make you weak; it makes you respected.

4. Listening is as important as speaking – Good manners include paying attention to others, not just waiting for your turn to talk.

5. Handling conflict with grace – People with good manners don't argue aggressively; they communicate with respect and maturity.

Practical Steps & Actionable Tips

1. Use "Please" and "Thank You" naturally – It shows appreciation and respect.

2. Make eye contact and smile – It builds confidence and trust.

3. Listen more than you speak – People appreciate being heard.

4. Respect people's time – Show up on time and value commitments.

5. Avoid interrupting – Give people space to express their thoughts.

6. Be mindful of digital etiquette – In today's world, replying politely, avoiding all-caps shouting, and respecting privacy matter.

7. Apologize when necessary – Owning up to mistakes shows maturity and strength.

Reflection Questions for the Reader

How do I want people to remember their interactions with me?

Do I listen attentively, or do I focus on what I'll say next?

When was the last time I showed kindness without expecting anything in return?

How do I handle disagreements? With respect or frustration?

Final Thought

Good manners cost nothing but bring huge returns in personal and professional life. They make people trust, respect, and remember you for the right reasons. If you cultivate good manners, you will stand out—not just for what you achieve, but for the way you treat others along the way.

III

Kindness – The Strength of a Gentle Heart

"No act of kindness, no matter how small, is ever wasted." – Aesop

Why Kindness Matters

Kindness is often underestimated. Many mistake it for weakness, thinking that only those who are aggressive or self-serving succeed. But true strength lies in kindness. It is not about being naive—it is about choosing to be compassionate even when it is easier to be indifferent.

In a world where competition is fierce and people are often focused on themselves, kindness is a rare and powerful trait. It builds trust, strengthens relationships, and opens doors to opportunities that arrogance never will. Whether in business, leadership, or personal life, the ability to treat people with warmth and generosity sets you apart.

Science supports this. Studies show that acts of kindness reduce stress, improve mental health, and even increase lifespan. More importantly, kindness is contagious—one act can inspire many, creating a ripple effect that benefits both individuals and society.

When you look at the most admired and respected people in history, you'll notice that they weren't just successful—they were also known for their kindness and ability to uplift others.

Real-Life Examples

Mahatma Gandhi: Leading with Kindness

Gandhi led India's independence movement through non-violence and compassion. He responded to oppression not with hatred, but with peace and moral strength. His approach inspired millions and changed the course of history. His legacy proves that true leadership is not about force—it is about inspiring change through kindness and conviction.

Keanu Reeves: A Celebrity with a Kind Heart

Despite his global fame, Keanu Reeves is known for his humility and generosity. He has quietly donated millions to hospitals, treated film crews with respect, and helped strangers without seeking attention. His success hasn't changed his character—he remains one of the most beloved actors not just for his talent, but for the way he treats people.

These examples show that kindness is not a weakness—it is a sign of true inner strength and integrity.

Key Lessons from Kindness

1. Kindness is remembered longer than success – People may forget your words or achievements, but they will always remember how you made them feel.

1. Being kind does not mean being weak – It takes strength to be kind in a world that can be harsh.

3. Kindness builds connections – The more kindness you show, the stronger your relationships become.

4. It costs nothing but gives everything – A kind act can change someone's entire day or even their life.

5. Kindness attracts opportunity – People naturally trust and want to work with those who are warm and respectful.

Practical Steps & Actionable Tips

1. Practice small acts of kindness daily – A kind word, a helping hand, or a smile can make a difference.

2. Be kind even when no one is watching – True kindness is not about recognition but about character.

3. Choose kindness over ego – When faced with a choice, choose to be kind rather than to prove you are right.

4. Help someone without expecting anything in return – The greatest kindness is given freely.

5. Listen with empathy – Kindness isn't just about actions—it's about truly listening and understanding others.

6. Forgive more often – Holding grudges only harms you; kindness includes letting go of past resentment.

7. Be kind to yourself – Self-kindness leads to confidence, happiness, and better mental health.

Reflection Questions for the Reader

When was the last time I did something kind for someone without expecting anything in return?

Do I choose kindness even when it is difficult?

Have I ever misjudged kindness as a weakness?

How can I be more intentional about kindness in my daily life?

Final Thought

Kindness has the power to transform lives, including your own. In a world where people are often self-focused, being kind makes you stand out as a leader, a friend, and a person of value. The strongest people are not those who dominate others, but those who uplift them.

The world does not need more successful people who lack kindness—it needs successful people who use their success to help others. Be one of them.

IV

Respect – The Foundation of Honor and Integrity

"Respect yourself and others will respect you." – Confucius

Why Respect Matters

Respect is the foundation of strong relationships, leadership, and personal integrity. It influences how we treat others, how we are treated in return, and ultimately, how we navigate life. A person who respects life, themselves, their family, elders, leaders, and God carries a sense of honor that shapes their decisions and interactions.

Respect is not just about manners or obedience—it is about recognition and appreciation. It means understanding the value of people, positions, traditions, and principles. It is what makes societies function, workplaces productive, and families strong.

A lack of respect leads to conflict, disconnection, and failure. When people fail to respect their parents, mentors, or even themselves, they drift without guidance, make poor choices, and struggle to build meaningful relationships. In contrast, those who cultivate respect earn trust, authority, and lasting success.

Real-Life Examples

Nelson Mandela: Respect as a Tool for Peace

Despite spending 27 years in prison, Mandela emerged with no bitterness, choosing respect and reconciliation over hatred. He respected even his former oppressors, understanding that true leadership is about unity, not revenge. His ability to treat others with dignity made him one of the most revered leaders of all time.

Michael Jordan: Self-Respect and Professionalism

Jordan, one of the greatest athletes in history, was known for his relentless self-respect. He respected his body by training intensely, respected the game by giving his best effort, and respected his team by leading with example. His commitment to excellence was rooted in respecting the process, the sport, and himself.

These figures show that respect is not submission—it is strength, wisdom, and a sign of a great leader.

Forms of Respect

1. Respect for Life – Every life has value; showing care for people, animals, and nature.

1. Respect for Parents – Honoring those who gave us life and guidance.

3. Respect for Elders – Recognizing wisdom and experience, learning from those before us.

4. Respect for Rank & Authority – Understanding hierarchy and the role of leadership.

5. Respect for Oneself – Carrying self-worth, setting boundaries, and striving for excellence.

6. Respect for Leaders – Whether in politics, faith, or business, leadership deserves acknowledgment.

7. Respect for God & Faith – For those who believe, respecting divine principles and values brings deeper meaning to life.

Key Lessons from Respect

1. Respect is earned, but it is also given – Treat others with dignity, and you will receive the same in return.

2. Self-respect leads to confidence – If you value yourself, you make better choices and avoid toxic influences.

3. Respecting authority does not mean blind obedience – It means acknowledging roles and responsibilities while maintaining your values.

4. Respect is the foundation of leadership – Those who treat others well naturally gain influence.

5. Respect brings peace and wisdom – It prevents unnecessary conflicts and fosters understanding.

Practical Steps & Actionable Tips

1. Show appreciation – Thank your parents, mentors, and elders for their guidance.

2. Listen before judging – Understand perspectives before reacting.

3. Maintain dignity in disagreements – Respect means arguing with logic, not insults.

4. Take care of yourself – Self-respect includes health, discipline, and personal standards.

5. Acknowledge people's efforts – Whether a CEO or a janitor, everyone deserves respect.

6. Stand for what is right – True respect includes integrity and speaking up when necessary.

7. Be mindful of cultural and religious beliefs – Respect different traditions and worldviews.

Reflection Questions for the Reader

Do I show respect to my family, teachers, and elders, even when we disagree?

How do I treat people with lower status or power than me?

Do I respect myself enough to make wise choices and set boundaries?

How do I handle authority—do I challenge it respectfully or rebel without purpose?

Do I show gratitude and honor to those who lead or guide me?

Final Thought

Respect is not just about words—it is about actions, attitude, and mindset. A respectful person gains influence, earns trust, and leaves a lasting impact. Whether in leadership, personal relationships, or self-growth, respect is the pillar that upholds true character and honor.

The world does not need more people who demand respect—it needs more people who give it freely and embody it in their daily lives. Be one of them.

V

Responsibility – The Foundation of Leadership, Trust, and Value

"The price of greatness is responsibility." – Winston Churchill

Why Responsibility Matters

Responsibility is not just about doing what is required—it is about ownership, accountability, and leadership. It is the foundation on which trust, success, and respect are built. Whether in personal life, career, business, or leadership, those who take responsibility are the ones who create real impact.

Responsibility is not limited to age, status, or position. A child is responsible for their actions, a student for their learning, an employee for their work, a leader for their decisions, and a parent for their family. Irrespective of your role, responsibility is a measure of maturity and strength. It is the bridge between trust and leadership—those who own their actions gain the trust of others and are seen as reliable and capable.

People who avoid responsibility blame others, make excuses, or shy away from commitments. But those who embrace it become the decision-makers, the problem-solvers, and the ones others look up to.

Real-Life Examples

George Washington: Leading by Example

Washington did not just fight for American independence—he took responsibility for leading a new nation. When he could have seized power, he stepped down after two terms as President, setting an example of leadership rooted in duty, not personal gain.

Simone Biles: Owning Her Well-Being

As one of the greatest gymnasts in history, Biles shocked the world when she withdrew from the 2021 Olympics, citing mental health concerns. Instead of pushing through recklessly, she took responsibility for her well-being, setting an example that health—physical and mental—is also a responsibility.

These examples prove that responsibility is not about doing everything alone, but about owning decisions, actions, and consequences.

Key Lessons from Responsibility

1. Trust is built on responsibility – The more responsible you are, the more people rely on you.

1. Taking responsibility gives you control – Blaming others keeps you powerless; owning your actions gives you power.

3. Responsibility is the foundation of leadership – No one follows someone who avoids accountability.

4. Your choices shape your life – Every decision has consequences; responsible people think ahead.

5. Responsibility includes self-care – Taking care of your health, mindset, and emotions is your duty, not an option.

Practical Steps & Actionable Tips

1. Own your mistakes – When you fail, admit it, learn, and improve.

2. Stop blaming and start solving – Complaining does nothing; responsible people focus on solutions.

3. Be reliable – Keep your commitments and follow through on promises.

4. Manage your time wisely – Irresponsibility often starts with poor time management.

5. Understand the weight of leadership – If you want to lead, you must take responsibility for outcomes.

6. Take care of yourself – You are responsible for your health, mindset, and growth.

7. Be proactive, not reactive – Anticipate problems and take action before they escalate.

Reflection Questions for the Reader

Do I take full responsibility for my choices, or do I shift blame?

Can people trust me to follow through on my commitments?

How do I handle failure—do I learn from it, or do I make excuses?

What area of my life do I need to take more responsibility for?

Final Thought

Responsibility is the foundation of trust, leadership, and value. The world does not need more people who avoid accountability—it needs people who take ownership of their actions and decisions. Those who embrace responsibility earn respect, build strong relationships, and create lasting success.

No matter your age or role, taking responsibility sets you apart as a person of integrity and reliability. If you want to lead, inspire, and be trusted—start by taking responsibility today.

VI

Encouragement – Fuel for the Journey

"A word of encouragement during a failure is worth more than an hour of praise after success."
– Unknown

Why Encouragement Matters

Encouragement is the fuel that keeps us moving forward, especially when the road is long and difficult. It is not a luxury—it is a necessity. No great achievement happens without hope, motivation, and the right people supporting you along the way.

Many underestimate encouragement, but the truth is discouragement can be a terminal illness. It can stop dreams before they begin. It can make talented people give up, not because they lack ability, but because they lack support. Encouragement is what keeps people fighting when the odds are against them. It reminds them that, no matter how far the destination seems, they will get there.

Imagine life as a long journey. You need the right vehicle and mode of transport to make it to your destination smoothly. That vehicle is built with self-belief, encouragement, and a strong support system. If you choose the wrong vehicle—negative self-talk, toxic people, or self-doubt—you may never reach where you are meant to go.

So the question is: Are you fueling your journey with encouragement or allowing discouragement to slow you down?

Real-Life Examples

Walt Disney: Believing Against All Odds

Disney was fired from a newspaper because he was told he "lacked creativity." He faced multiple business failures before building his empire. But he never gave up. He surrounded himself with people who believed in his vision, and because of that, the world has Disney today.

Cristiano Ronaldo: Rising Above Doubt

As a young boy, Ronaldo was told he was too thin and weak to play professional football. Instead of giving in to discouragement, he used it as motivation. He trained harder, surrounded himself with coaches and mentors who believed in him, and built himself into one of the greatest footballers of all time.

These stories show that encouragement is the difference between quitting and persisting.

Key Lessons from Encouragement

1. Your environment matters – Surround yourself with uplifting people who push you forward.

1. Discouragement is poison – Learn to recognize and remove negative influences.

3. Hope is stronger than fear – No matter how far the goal seems, you will get there if you keep moving.

4. Choose the right vehicle – Fill your mind with positive reinforcement, good mentors, and belief in yourself.

5. Be an encourager – Just as you need encouragement, others do too. Give it freely.

Practical Steps & Actionable Tips

1. Avoid toxic people – If someone constantly discourages you, create distance.

2. Find your encouragers – Seek mentors, friends, and colleagues who inspire and uplift you.

3. Use positive self-talk – Be your own biggest supporter.

4. Celebrate small wins – Each step forward is progress. Recognize it.

5. Read biographies of overcomers – Learn from those who refused to give up.

6. Encourage others – The more you uplift others, the more encouragement comes back to you.

7. Keep your eyes on the destination – The journey may be long, but success is inevitable if you keep going.

Reflection Questions for the Reader

Who in my life encourages me, and who discourages me?

How do I respond to setbacks—do I give up or push forward?

Do I surround myself with people who believe in my journey?

Am I an encourager to others?

Final Thought

No matter how far away success seems, you will get there if you keep moving forward. The journey may have obstacles, but the key is choosing the right vehicle—a mindset of encouragement, resilience, and positivity. Surround yourself with the right people, reject discouragement, and fuel your journey with belief.

You are capable. You are worthy. Keep going.

VII

Discipline – The Foundation of Growth and Leadership

"We must all suffer one of two things: the pain of discipline or the pain of regret." – Jim Rohn

Why Discipline Matters

Discipline is the bridge between goals and achievements. It is what separates those who dream from those who succeed. While talent and intelligence can give you an advantage, it is discipline that sustains long-term success.

Discipline is about staying the course, even when progress seems slow or difficult. It is about trusting the process, understanding that the biggest rewards come not from easy shortcuts, but from doing the hard things first.

This is what builds strength, resilience, and character.

The truth is, discipline makes life easier in the long run. If you choose discipline today—whether in your work, health, or personal development—you will eventually see exponential growth. What seems hard at first becomes second nature, and the success that once felt distant will feel inevitable.

In leadership, discipline instills confidence in others. A disciplined leader is reliable, stable, and consistent. Teams trust those who show self-control, follow through on commitments, and set an example through action.

Real-Life Examples

Kobe Bryant: The Mamba Mentality

Kobe Bryant was known for his extreme work ethic. While others rested, he trained harder, doing the difficult work before it became easy. His discipline set him apart and made him one of the greatest basketball players of all time. His teammates respected him, not just for his talent, but for his unwavering dedication.

Elon Musk: Relentless Work Ethic

Musk has built multiple billion-dollar companies, not because he was the smartest person in the room, but because of his disciplined approach to problem-solving and execution. He works long hours, remains focused on the mission, and consistently delivers on impossible goals. His teams follow him because they trust his discipline and vision.

These examples show that discipline is not just about personal success—it builds trust, stability, and leadership.

Key Lessons from Discipline

1. Do the hard things first – The biggest growth happens when you tackle challenges head-on.

1. Trust the process – Progress may seem slow, but discipline compounds over time.

3. Discipline creates freedom – When you master self-control, you control your future.

4. Consistency builds confidence – People trust those who show up, deliver, and remain stable.

5. Shortcuts weaken character – Those who avoid discipline now will struggle later.

Practical Steps & Actionable Tips

1. Build daily habits – Small, consistent actions lead to massive results.

2. Prioritize hard tasks – Do the most difficult work first when energy is highest.

3. Eliminate distractions – Stay focused on what truly matters.

4. Set clear goals – Discipline thrives on purpose and direction.

5. Stay accountable – Find mentors, coaches, or routines that keep you on track.

6. Be patient – Growth is slow at first, but discipline accelerates results over time.

7. Lead by example – If you want others to trust you, show discipline in your own life.

Reflection Questions for the Reader

Do I have the discipline to stay committed even when things get hard?

Am I prioritizing long-term success over short-term comfort?

How do I handle setbacks—do I stay the course or give up too soon?

What habits can I develop today to strengthen my discipline?

Final Thought

Discipline is not about punishment—it is about freedom, strength, and mastery. If you build discipline in small ways today, you will reap massive rewards in the future. Success, leadership, and trust are not built overnight—they come from consistent effort, stability, and doing the hard things first.

The world follows those who are disciplined because they create certainty in an uncertain world. Be one of them.

VIII

Resilience – Built to Last

"When the going gets tough, the tough get going." – Joseph P. Kennedy

Why Resilience Matters

Life is not a straight road. It is filled with unexpected challenges, failures, and setbacks. The difference between those who succeed and those who don't is not just talent, luck, or intelligence—it is resilience.

Resilience is the ability to bounce back, push forward, and keep going no matter how tough things get. It is what separates champions from the rest. The most unforgettable victories happen in the final moments—the last-second goals, the game-winning shots, the comebacks that seemed impossible. These moments happen because some people refuse to quit, no matter the odds.

Think of how many times in history people have been counted out, told they wouldn't make it, only to rise from the ashes and prove everyone wrong. Resilience is what makes that possible.

If you want to succeed in life, business, sports, or personal growth, you need to develop the mindset that says:

"I will not give up."

"No matter how many times I fall, I will get back up."

"I will outlast the struggle."

Your ability to endure when things get tough will determine how far you go. The ones who last are the ones who win.

Real-Life Examples

Michael Jordan: The Power of a Comeback

Michael Jordan is widely considered the greatest basketball player of all time. But before he became a legend, he was cut from his high school basketball team. Instead of quitting, he trained harder, pushed himself beyond limits, and came back stronger.

His career is filled with last-second, game-winning shots, but they were not just moments of luck. Jordan created those moments through years of resilient discipline and mental toughness. His famous shot in Game 6 of the 1998 NBA Finals sealed his legacy as a player who never backed down when the pressure was on.

J.K. Rowling: Rejected But Never Defeated

Before she became a household name, J.K. Rowling faced 12 rejections from publishers for

Harry Potter. Many people would have given up after the first few failures. She didn't. She kept pushing forward, believing in her work, until one publisher finally said yes. Today, Harry Potter is one of the best-selling book series in history, all because she refused to give up.

These stories prove that resilience is the key to lasting success.

Key Lessons from Resilience

1. The game is never over until you decide it is – Even in the final moments, a comeback is possible.

1. Failure is not the end—it's a lesson – Every setback is a setup for a stronger comeback.

3. Resilience is built, not given – It grows every time you push through challenges.

4. Pressure creates champions – The hardest moments test and refine you.

5. You only lose if you stop trying – Keep going, and success will come.

Practical Steps & Actionable Tips

1. Embrace setbacks as fuel – Every failure is part of the process. Learn from it.

2. Develop a never-give-up mindset – Train yourself to see obstacles as challenges, not dead ends.

3. Push through discomfort – The biggest breakthroughs come after the hardest struggles.

4. Visualize your comeback – Just like athletes visualize winning moments, see yourself overcoming the odds.

5. Surround yourself with resilient people – Find mentors and friends who inspire perseverance.

6. Control what you can, accept what you can't – Focus on actions, not excuses.

7. Stay in the game – Success often comes to those who outlast their competition.

Why Last-Second Victories Matter

There's a reason sports fans remember last-second goals and buzzer-beaters. Those moments teach us that you are never truly out of the game until the final whistle blows.

Think of:

Liverpool's Miracle in Istanbul (2005 UEFA Champions League Final) – Down 3-0 at halftime, Liverpool staged one of the greatest comebacks in football history, proving that resilience can turn defeat into triumph.

Tom Brady's Super Bowl Comeback (2017) – The New England Patriots trailed 28-3 before launching the biggest comeback in Super Bowl history. Brady and his team never lost faith, and they secured a victory that no one thought possible.

LeBron James in the 2016 NBA Finals – The Cleveland Cavaliers were down 3-1 in the series but fought back to defeat the Golden State Warriors, proving that a champion is never truly beaten until they quit.

These moments are not just about sports—they are about life. Success often happens at the moment when most people would have given up.

Reflection Questions for the Reader

Have I ever given up too soon? What would have happened if I had pushed through?

What challenges in my life are testing my resilience right now?

How can I reframe failures as stepping stones instead of setbacks?

Do I surround myself with people who encourage me to keep going?

Final Thought

Resilience is what separates those who almost made it from those who actually do. The world is filled with people who gave up when success was just around the corner. Don't be one of them.

When life gets tough, when the pressure is on, and when the odds are against you—remember that the greatest victories happen in the final moments. Stay in the game, keep taking the shots, and never give up.

You are built to last.

IX

Perseverance – The Power of Pushing Forward

"It does not matter how slowly you go as long as you do not stop." – Confucius

Why Perseverance Matters

Perseverance is the ability to keep moving forward despite obstacles, failures, and fatigue. It is different from resilience—while resilience is about bouncing back from setbacks, perseverance is about pushing forward even when success feels distant.

If resilience is about making comebacks, perseverance is about endurance. It is what keeps a marathon runner going after 30 kilometers when their legs feel like giving up. It is what makes an entrepreneur hold onto their vision after years of setbacks. It is what separates those who almost made it from those who finally do.

Perseverance is not just about effort—it is about long-term commitment. Whether in sports, business, or personal growth, those who succeed are not necessarily the most talented, but the ones who keep going when others quit.

Real-Life Examples

Marathon Runners: Endurance is Key

A marathon is 42.2 kilometers of physical and mental battle. The toughest part comes after 30 kilometers when exhaustion sets in. Many runners hit the "wall", a moment when their body begs them to stop. But those who push through the pain, who refuse to quit, who take one step at a time—those are the ones who finish.

Eliud Kipchoge, the world's greatest marathon runner, made history by running a marathon in under two hours—a feat once thought impossible. He didn't achieve it overnight. It took years of disciplined perseverance, training through discomfort, and believing in what others doubted.

Ironman Competitions: The Ultimate Test of Perseverance

An Ironman triathlon consists of a 3.8 km swim, 180 km cycling, and a full marathon (42.2 km)—all in one race. Completing it requires extraordinary perseverance, not just physical but mental. Many competitors struggle, cramp, and nearly collapse, but those who finish are proof that determination beats exhaustion.

Chris Nikic, the first athlete with Down syndrome to complete an Ironman, is a perfect example of perseverance. Doctors once said he would struggle with coordination and endurance. But he proved them wrong by training relentlessly, refusing to give up, and crossing the finish line against all odds.

Industry Example: Dyson's 5,126 Failures

James Dyson, the inventor of the Dyson vacuum cleaner, failed 5,126 times before creating a successful prototype. For 15 years, he kept going, despite rejection, financial struggles, and people doubting him. Today, Dyson is a billion-dollar company, all because its founder never quit.

These examples prove that those who persevere—even when success seems impossible—are the ones who change the world.

Key Lessons from Perseverance

1. Perseverance is not about speed—it's about endurance – Just like in a marathon, winning is about lasting, not rushing.

1. Pain is temporary, quitting is forever – Every challenge will pass, but giving up means losing what could have been.

3. Success comes to those who stay in the race – Many great achievers were once on the edge of giving up, but they pushed through.

4. Belief fuels perseverance – If you believe in the destination, you will find the strength to keep going.

5. Every struggle is part of the process – The difficulties you face are shaping you into the person who can achieve your goal.

Practical Steps & Actionable Tips

1. Take it one step at a time – If you can't see the finish line, just focus on the next step.

2. Train yourself to keep going – Just like endurance athletes build stamina, train your mind to push through obstacles.

3. Reframe failures as progress – Every failure is a lesson, and every setback is a step forward.

4. Surround yourself with perseverance-minded people – The right environment will keep you going when motivation runs low.

5. Develop a "never quit" mindset – The moment you want to give up is the moment perseverance matters most.

6. Celebrate small victories – Acknowledge progress, even if you're not at the finish line yet.

7. Trust the process – Success takes time. Stay patient and keep pushing forward.

Reflection Questions for the Reader

Have I ever given up too soon? How would my life be different if I had kept going?

What is one challenge I need to persevere through right now?

Do I view setbacks as signs to quit or as opportunities to grow?

How can I strengthen my perseverance and endurance mindset?

Final Thought

Perseverance is what turns the impossible into reality. Whether in sports, business, or personal life, those who refuse to quit are the ones who achieve greatness.

Like a marathon runner who pushes through exhaustion, like an entrepreneur who keeps innovating despite failures, like an athlete who fights until the final second—those who persevere are the ones who win in the end.

You don't have to be the fastest or the strongest. You just have to keep moving forward.

"If you can't fly, then run. If you can't run, then walk. If you can't walk, then crawl. But whatever you do, you have to keep moving forward." – Martin Luther King Jr.

X

Gratitude – The Art of Appreciating Life

"Gratitude turns what we have into enough." – Anonymous

Why Gratitude Matters

In the rush of daily life, we often forget to pause and appreciate the simple yet profound blessings that surround us. We chase after success, significance, and impact, yet sometimes, the greatest fulfillment comes not from what we achieve but from what we acknowledge and appreciate.

Gratitude is not just saying "thank you"—it is a way of seeing life. It is about recognizing the miracle of existence, the kindness of others, and the beauty of a world we often take for granted. It reminds us that no matter how challenging life gets, there is always something to be thankful for.

Being truly grateful means appreciating everything—from the breath we take to the people who shape our lives, from the opportunities before us to the sacrifices made by those who came before us. It is in gratitude that we find deeper meaning, peace, and a profound sense of belonging.

Gratitude for the Pillars of Our Lives

1. **Gratitude to God** – Regardless of belief, acknowledging a higher power or purpose brings humility and peace. Life is a gift, and every new day is another chance to do something meaningful.

1. **Gratitude to Family** – Our parents, siblings, and extended family are our first teachers, protectors, and supporters. They may not be perfect, but their presence shapes who we are.

3. **Gratitude to Friends** – True friends stand by us through life's highs and lows. A single, genuine friend is more valuable than a hundred acquaintances.

4. **Gratitude to Teachers & Mentors** – The knowledge we have, the skills we develop, and the wisdom we gain are because of those who took the time to teach and guide us.

5. **Gratitude to the Nation & Forefathers** – The freedoms, security, and opportunities we enjoy are because of the sacrifices of those who came before us. Recognizing their struggles and contributions instills responsibility

in us to build a better future.

6. **Gratitude for Health** – The simple ability to breathe, walk, see, and experience life is a gift we often overlook until it is threatened. Our bodies are miraculous, and taking care of them is an act of gratitude.

7. **Gratitude for the Beauty Around Us** – The sky, the oceans, the forests, the laughter of children, the kindness of strangers—the world is filled with beauty that we often fail to notice.

Real-Life Examples

Nick Vujicic: Gratitude Without Limits

Born without arms and legs, Nick Vujicic could have easily lived in bitterness. Instead, he chose gratitude—focusing on what he could do rather than what he lacked. Today, he inspires millions as a speaker, showing that gratitude transforms challenges into strengths.

Nelson Mandela: Gratitude in Adversity

After spending 27 years in prison, Mandela emerged without resentment. He chose gratitude over hatred, acknowledging that every experience—even the painful ones—contributed to a greater purpose. His gratitude led to reconciliation, not revenge.

These stories prove that gratitude is not about having everything—it is about appreciating everything.

Key Lessons from Gratitude

1. Gratitude brings fulfillment – Happiness does not come from getting more but from appreciating what you already have.

2. What you focus on grows – If you focus on problems, they will multiply. If you focus on gratitude, blessings will multiply.

3. Gratitude strengthens relationships – People love to be around those who appreciate them.

4. Being grateful makes you resilient – Those who practice gratitude recover faster from setbacks.

5. Gratitude shifts perspective – When you count your blessings, life feels richer, not poorer.

Practical Steps & Actionable Tips

1. Start a gratitude journal – Write three things you are grateful for every day.

2. Express appreciation to people – Say "thank you" more often, whether to family, friends, or colleagues.

3. Notice the little things – The sunrise, a kind word, a good meal—appreciate the small joys.

4. Give back – The best way to show gratitude is to share your blessings.

5. Change "I have to" into "I get to" – Instead of "I have to work," say, "I get to work and provide for my family."

6. Practice gratitude in tough times – Even in hardship, find something to appreciate.

7. Limit complaints – The less you complain, the more you see the good around you.

Reflection Questions for the Reader

Do I focus more on what I lack or what I have?
When was the last time I expressed deep gratitude to someone?
How can I incorporate gratitude into my daily life?
What are three things I am grateful for right now?

Final Thought

Gratitude is not about having everything—it is about recognizing everything you already have. It turns simple moments into extraordinary ones and transforms struggles into wisdom.

If you want a life of meaning and fulfillment, start by being grateful for the breath you take, the people around you, and the opportunities before you. The world is beautiful—don't ignore it. Appreciate it.

XI

Financial Awareness – Mastering Money in a World of Distractions

"Do not save what is left after spending, but spend what is left after saving." – Warren Buffett

Why Financial Awareness Matters

We live in a world where money flows faster than ever, not just in reality but in perception. Social media platforms like Instagram, TikTok, and YouTube have reshaped how we think about money, making luxury lifestyles look like the norm and subtly influencing our financial decisions. Every day, we are bombarded with targeted ads, influencer promotions, and marketing strategies that are designed to control our spending.

The world no longer just sells products—it sells lifestyles, making us believe that we need to spend to keep up. The problem? Most people don't even realize they are being influenced. This leads to impulse buying, excessive debt, poor savings habits, and financial instability.

To build a strong financial foundation, you must develop financial awareness—knowing where your money goes, why you spend, and how to make money work for you instead of against you.

The Battle Between Needs, Wants, and Waste

One of the biggest financial mistakes people make is failing to distinguish between:

Needs – Essentials required for survival and stability (food, housing, healthcare).

Wants – Things that add comfort and enjoyment but are not necessary.

Waste – Unnecessary spending that drains financial resources without adding value.

Most people live paycheck to paycheck because they confuse wants with needs and waste money without realizing it. The key to financial security is to prioritize needs, control wants, and eliminate waste.

Short-Term Gratification vs. Long-Term Stability

Social media conditions people for instant gratification—quick purchases, fast dopamine hits, and the illusion of wealth. But true financial success comes from delayed gratification and long-term planning.

Buying the latest gadgets every year = short-term gratification

Investing in assets that grow in value over time = long-term stability

The wealthy build assets (things that generate income), while most people accumulate liabilities (things that drain money). Ask yourself: Am I building wealth or just spending?

Key Financial Principles for Personal Wealth

1. Live Below Your Means – If you earn $5,000 a month but spend $5,500, you are digging a financial hole. Spend less than you earn and save the difference.

1. Track Every Dollar – If you don't know where your money is going, you are already losing it. Use budgeting apps or a simple notebook to track income and expenses.

3. Save First, Spend Later – Set aside at least 20% of your income before spending on anything else. Make saving a habit, not an afterthought.

4. Invest Wisely – Money in a savings account loses value due to inflation. Invest in stocks, mutual funds, real estate, or businesses that grow over time.

5. Avoid Debt Traps – Credit cards, personal loans, and high-interest payments can enslave you for years. If you can't buy it with cash, think twice before using credit.

6. Have an Emergency Fund – Set aside 3-6 months' worth of expenses in a separate account to handle unexpected crises without going into debt.

7. Understand Risk – Every investment carries risks. Don't invest blindly—educate yourself first.

Financial Discipline in Business

Personal finance is one thing, but if you're running a business, financial discipline is the backbone of success. Many businesses fail, not because the idea was bad, but because financial mismanagement drained resources.

Key Financial Principles for Business Success

1. Separate Business and Personal Finances – Never mix them. Keep separate accounts to track business cash flow.

2. Monitor and Forecast Cash Flow – Many businesses fail because they run out of cash. Always know how much is coming in and going out.

3. Invest in Growth, Not Lifestyle – Business owners who spend profits on luxury instead of reinvesting in growth often collapse.

4. Keep Operating Costs Low – A lean business survives longer. Avoid unnecessary expenses and optimize resources.

5. Know Your Break-Even Point – Understand how much revenue is needed to cover costs before making a profit.

6. Limit Debt and Maintain Liquidity – A business that relies too much on debt is always one crisis away from collapse.

Avoiding Financial Pitfalls

1. The Debt Trap – Credit card debt, personal loans, payday loans—they keep you paying forever while enriching banks and lenders. Avoid debt unless it is for a meaningful investment (such as property or education).

2. Lifestyle Inflation – When income increases, people increase their spending instead of their savings. This leads to an endless cycle of earning more but never feeling financially secure.

3. The "Keeping Up" Mentality – Just because influencers and celebrities show off luxury lifestyles on social media does not mean they are financially stable. Many are drowning in debt behind the scenes. Live for yourself, not for appearances.

4. Not Having a Financial Plan – Without a plan, money flows aimlessly. Set financial goals for the next 5, 10, and

20 years. Know where you want to go financially.

Practical Steps & Actionable Tips

1. Create a Budget – List your income and expenses and set limits for each category.

2. Automate Savings – Set up an automatic transfer to a savings or investment account every month.

3. Read Financial Books – Learn from experts like Warren Buffett, Robert Kiyosaki, and Dave Ramsey.

4. Avoid Unnecessary Subscriptions – Streaming services, memberships, and impulse purchases add up quickly.

5. Invest Early – Even small amounts invested today will multiply over decades.

6. Check Your Credit Score Regularly – A good credit score helps with lower interest rates and financial opportunities.

7. Practice Financial Minimalism – Buy only what adds real value to your life.

Reflection Questions for the Reader

Do I control my money, or does my money control me? Am I building wealth, or just spending?

What financial habits do I need to change right now?

How can I avoid the financial traps that many people fall into?

Final Thought

Money is a powerful tool—it can either build your future or trap you in endless debt. Financial awareness is about knowing the difference between wise spending and impulsive decisions, between investments and expenses, between needs and wants.

In a world filled with marketing distractions, true financial freedom comes from knowledge, discipline, and intentionality. If you want a better future, start controlling your finances today.

XII

Healthy Habits – Building a Strong Foundation for Life in the Digital Age

"We are what we repeatedly do. Excellence, then, is not an act, but a habit." – Aristotle

Why Healthy Habits Matter More Than Ever

Success is not built overnight. It is the result of daily habits that strengthen the mind, body, and spirit. Many people believe that hard work alone determines success, but in reality, it is disciplined habits that create long-term results.

However, in today's digital age, forming and maintaining healthy habits is harder than ever. Social media, video games, endless streaming, and digital distractions pull people into a vortex of passive consumption. Many wake up scrolling mindlessly, lose track of time in cyber-worlds, and struggle to stay present in the real world.

Technology is a powerful tool, but if used poorly, it controls you instead of empowering you. The challenge today is not just about building discipline but resisting distractions and staying present.

Healthy habits build focus, character, and resilience—all necessary for a successful life. By working on physical, mental, and spiritual health while controlling digital distractions, you can build a life of real growth and fulfillment.

The Three Pillars of Healthy Habits

1. Physical Health – Strength for the Journey

Your body is the vehicle that carries you through life. If it is weak or neglected, everything else suffers.

Exercise daily – Whether it's walking, strength training, or yoga, movement fuels energy.

Eat real food – Avoid processed junk. Nutrition directly affects mood, focus, and longevity.

Sleep with discipline – No achievement is worth sacrificing long-term health. Aim for 7-8 hours of quality sleep.

Stay hydrated – Proper hydration boosts energy and mental clarity.

Avoid addictive habits – Excess caffeine, smoking, alcohol, and junk food create long-term health issues.

Example: Tom Brady remains one of the greatest athletes at 46 due to his commitment to strict nutrition, disciplined workouts, and recovery habits.

2. Mental Health – Your Strongest Weapon

Your mind is your greatest asset or your biggest weakness. Healthy habits sharpen focus, reduce stress, and build resilience.

Read and learn daily – Expand your thinking with books, podcasts, and skill-building.

Control your information diet – Avoid excessive news, negativity, and toxic online content.

Practice mindfulness – Whether through meditation, journaling, or reflection, create space for mental clarity.

Stay socially connected – Real relationships bring happiness, not likes or comments.

Develop mental toughness – Challenges will come, but those who train their minds to stay focused will succeed.

Example: Bill Gates schedules "Think Weeks," where he isolates himself from distractions to reflect, strategize, and read deeply. This habit fuels his success and sharp decision-making.

3. Spiritual Health – The Anchor in a Chaotic World

Spiritual health keeps people grounded, peaceful, and purposeful. In a world driven by material success, inner peace is often overlooked but is the key to lasting fulfillment.

Practice gratitude – Appreciate life's blessings rather than focusing on what's missing.

Have quiet time – Whether it's prayer, meditation, or stillness, find time for self-reflection.

Serve others – Helping people brings a sense of fulfillment that money cannot buy.

Live by principles – A meaningful life is built on values, not just achievements.

Example: Mahatma Gandhi's daily prayer and meditation strengthened his resolve, helping him lead India's independence movement through peace and perseverance.

How to Control Digital Distractions and Stay Present

The modern world is built for distraction. Apps, social media, and online platforms are designed to keep you addicted, pulling you into endless scrolling, mindless gaming, and digital escapism. If you don't control it, it will control you.

How to Break Free from the Digital Abyss

1. Limit Screen Time – Set strict time limits for social media, gaming, and entertainment apps. Use apps like Freedom or Moment to track usage.

1. Turn Off Notifications – Every beep, buzz, and alert is a hook for your attention. Disable unnecessary notifications.

3. Set No-Phone Zones – Keep your phone away during meals, conversations, and before bed.

4. Have Digital Detox Days – Take at least one day per week to unplug from unnecessary technology.

5. Replace Scrolling with Learning – Swap 30 minutes of social media with reading, skill-building, or meaningful conversations.

6. Stay Present in Real Life – Practice active listening, mindful conversations, and in-person interactions.

7. Use Social Media with Purpose – If it doesn't educate, inspire, or add value, limit your time on it.

Example: Top CEOs and successful leaders have strict digital boundaries—many don't check emails after work hours, limit social media, and dedicate time for deep work without distractions.

Key Healthy Habits for a Balanced Life

1. Own your mornings – Start the day with exercise, reflection, or learning—not scrolling.

2. Plan your time – A scheduled life leads to purpose-driven productivity.

3. Prioritize real-world experiences – Travel, explore, and interact with the real world instead of just consuming online content.

4. Say no to distractions – Avoid unnecessary notifications, emails, and low-value tasks.

5. Be consistent – The smallest good habits, when repeated daily, lead to massive long-term results.

Reflection Questions for the Reader

Are my daily habits helping or harming my long-term success?

How much time do I waste on social media and gaming?

What one digital habit can I change today for a healthier lifestyle?

Am I present in the real world, or am I living in a digital bubble?

Final Thought

Your habits shape your future. In the digital age, the ability to focus, avoid distractions, and maintain discipline is more valuable than ever. Technology can be an ally or an enemy—it depends on how you use it.

By balancing physical, mental, and spiritual health while staying present in the real world, you will unlock your full potential. The world is vast, beautiful, and full of real experiences—don't waste it being stuck behind a screen.

Live intentionally. Create habits that empower your future.

XIII

Success – A Life Rich in Experience

"Success is not final, failure is not fatal: it is the courage to continue that counts." – Winston Churchill

What is True Success?

Most people misunderstand success. They see it as a number in a bank account, a title on a business card, or a collection of material possessions. But real success is much deeper, richer, and more complex.

Success is not a moment—it is a lifetime of experiences, struggles, lessons, and contributions. It is about the journey, the endurance, and the impact you leave behind.

Look at history. Great achievements are celebrated in seconds, but they are built over years of dedication, discipline, and sacrifice.

A 100-meter race lasts 10 seconds, but it takes at least six years of training and countless races to get there.

A Nobel Prize moment lasts minutes, but it represents decades of research and perseverance.

A standing ovation after a performance lasts moments, but the artist has trained for a lifetime.

The reality

Success is not instant—it is built through pain, suffering, sacrifice, and persistence.

The Journey is Not Fun, Not Dull—It's Meaningful

Success is not just about enjoying life, nor is it about suffering endlessly. It is about embracing the journey—the highs, the lows, and everything in between.

Many people seek shortcuts, believing success should come quickly and easily. But the truth is:

There is no lasting success without hard work.

There is no achievement without sacrifice.

There is no growth without struggle.

The journey to success is neither pure fun nor completely dull—it is a mix of effort, passion, exhaustion, and joy. The people who succeed are the ones who accept this and keep moving forward, no matter how difficult it gets.

Success is Not Just Money or Wealth

Many define success by how much money they make or what they own, but true success is never just about wealth. If money were the only measure, then the richest people would be the happiest—but they are not.

Instead, true success includes:

1. Health Matters – A life of wealth without health is meaningless. Take care of your body and mind.

1. Family Matters – The greatest joy comes from relationships, not material things. Success means building strong bonds with family.

3. People You Influenced & Helped Matter – Who have you mentored, uplifted, or guided? Success is leaving people better than you found them.

4. Your Impact on the World & Community Matters – Have you contributed positively to your society, environment, and the people around you?

5. Legacy Matters – What will remain when you are gone? A successful life is one where your ideas, values, and kindness live on in others.

Example: Steve Jobs built Apple, but beyond money, his legacy is in how he changed technology, design, and the way we interact with the world.

Key Lessons from Success

1. Success is a marathon, not a sprint – The greatest victories take years of dedication.

2. Pain and suffering are part of the journey – No one succeeds without setbacks.

3. Success is measured by impact, not income – Who you help and influence matters more than how much you earn.

4. Legacy is greater than status – What you leave behind is the real measure of success.

5. Balance is key – Health, relationships, and purpose matter just as much as achievements.

Practical Steps & Actionable Tips

1. Define Your Own Success – Don't let society or social media tell you what success is. Decide what truly matters to you.

2. Stay Patient and Committed – Success is built over years, not days. Stay focused on the long-term goal.

3. Invest in Health and Relationships – A truly successful life is balanced between career, health, and family.

4. Give Back – Help others along the way. True leaders lift others as they rise.

5. Stay Grounded – No matter how much you achieve, stay humble. Success without character is empty.

6. Think Beyond Yourself – What legacy will you leave? Work on something that outlives you.

7. Enjoy the Process – Learn to love the journey. The struggle is part of the reward.

Reflection Questions for the Reader

Do I define success by money, or by meaning and impact?

Am I willing to endure the journey, or am I only chasing quick results?

Have I focused on relationships, health, and purpose, or just achievements?

What legacy am I building right now?

Final Thought

Success is not a moment—it is a lifetime of experiences, growth, and impact.

The real question is not "How much did you earn?", but "How many lives did you touch?". Not "How high did you climb?", but "Who did you lift up along the way?".

A truly successful life is one that leaves the world better than you found it.

Make your journey meaningful.

XIV

Applying These Lessons – Turning Knowledge into Action

"Knowing is not enough; we must apply. Willing is not enough; we must do." – Johann Wolfgang von Goethe

Why Application Matters

Reading, learning, and understanding principles are important, but without application, they mean nothing. Many people consume books, watch motivational speeches, and take courses, yet see no real change in their lives. Why? Because they don't apply what they learn.

Application is where the real transformation happens. The key to success is turning knowledge into action, making it practical, measurable, and achievable.

This chapter will help you:

- Take simple, fun, and practical steps to apply these lessons.
- Use SMART goals to track progress and stay consistent.
- Create a system for lifelong growth and improvement.

Let's make these lessons a part of your daily life in a way that is easy, rewarding, and sustainable.

The SMART Way to Apply What You Learn

A goal without a plan is just a wish. The best way to apply new habits is to follow the SMART framework:

S – Specific: Clearly define what you want to achieve.

M – Measurable: Track your progress with numbers.

A – Achievable: Make sure it is realistic.

R – Relevant: The goal should align with your bigger vision.

T – Time-bound: Set a clear deadline.

Example: Instead of saying "I want to be healthier," set a SMART goal:

✓ "I will walk 5,000 steps daily for the next 30 days and increase to 10,000 steps after that."

This makes the goal specific, measurable, achievable, relevant, and time-bound—increasing the chances of success.

Applying Key Lessons from This Book

1.

Success – Focus on the Journey, Not Just the Result

SMART Goal Example: Instead of saying, "I want to be successful," define it:

✓ "I will wake up at 6 AM every day, exercise for 30 minutes, and work on my personal growth for 1 hour."

Daily Action: Break long-term goals into daily habits that build momentum.

2.

Discipline – Small Steps Every Day

SMART Goal Example: Instead of saying, "I need to be more disciplined," say: ✓ "I will wake up at 6 AM for the next 21 days and not hit snooze."

Daily Action: Use a habit tracker or calendar to mark every day you stay consistent.

Example: Athletes and musicians practice daily—small efforts add up to greatness over time.

3.

Financial Awareness – Track and Control Your Money

SMART Goal Example: Instead of "I want to save money," be specific:

✓ "I will save $100 per month and invest 20% of my income in index funds."

Daily Action: Use a finance app to track expenses, limit impulse purchases, and automate savings.

Example: Warren Buffett built wealth not by earning more, but by spending wisely and investing consistently.

4. Healthy Habits – Balance in the Digital Age

SMART Goal Example: Instead of "I will stop wasting time on social media," say:

✓ "I will limit Instagram and TikTok to 30 minutes daily and use the extra time for reading."

Daily Action: Set screen time limits on your phone or use apps like Freedom or Forest to reduce distractions.

Example: Many successful people limit screen time, including Bill Gates and Jeff Bezos. Being present in real life matters.

5. Resilience – Embracing Failure as a Lesson

SMART Goal Example: Instead of "I will stop fearing failure," say:

✓ "I will apply for 10 jobs this month, knowing that rejection is part of the process."

Daily Action: When something doesn't go as planned, write down what you learned instead of feeling defeated.

Example: Michael Jordan was cut from his high school basketball team but didn't give up—he used failure as fuel for growth.

6. Building a Legacy – Making an Impact Beyond Yourself

SMART Goal Example: Instead of saying, "I want to leave a legacy," start with:

- "I will mentor one person in my community and teach them a skill every month."

Daily Action: Help others, give back, and share knowledge. Legacy is built through small actions over time.

Example: Nelson Mandela's legacy was not built in one speech—it was built through consistent action over decades.

Making It Fun and Sustainable

Many people fail to maintain new habits because they make them too difficult or boring. Here's how to make personal growth fun and sustainable:

- Gamify Progress: Create challenges (e.g., a 30-day fitness or reading challenge). ✓ Reward Yourself: Celebrate small wins (e.g., if you complete a goal, treat yourself to something enjoyable).
- Find Accountability Partners: Share goals with a friend, mentor, or coach to stay motivated. ✓ Mix It Up: Avoid burnout by keeping things fresh—learn new skills, try different workout routines, or explore new books.
- Use the 2-Minute Rule: If a task feels overwhelming, start with just 2 minutes (e.g., "I will read just one page"). Often, you'll keep going beyond that.

Tracking Progress and Staying Consistent

- Keep a Journal: Write down your goals, progress, and reflections.
- Use a Habit Tracker: Mark an 'X' on the calendar every day you complete a habit.
- Measure Progress Monthly: Review what's working and adjust where needed.
- Celebrate Milestones: Recognize and appreciate how far you've come.

Example: Marathon runners track every run, improving gradually over months and years. Progress is not instant, but measured growth leads to big success.

Reflection Questions for the Reader

Which one lesson from this book will I apply first?
What small daily action can I take today?
How will I track progress to stay accountable?
What will I do when I face setbacks—give up or adjust my approach?

Final Thought

Knowledge alone doesn't change lives—action does. What you do today shapes who you become tomorrow.

Success isn't about making perfect choices. It's about showing up, being consistent, and taking small steps daily. Whether it's financial success, better health, stronger relationships, or lasting impact, the principles in this book only work if you apply them.

So start today. Set a goal, take action, track progress, and keep going.

Because the future belongs to those who act.

XV

What to Avoid – A Warning Bell for Life's Hidden Traps

"A fool learns from his own mistakes. A wise man learns from the mistakes of others." – Otto von Bismarck

Why This Chapter Matters

Life is full of opportunities, but it is also full of traps, distractions, and dangers—some obvious, some hidden. Some mistakes can be recovered from, but others can destroy your future, relationships, and even your life.

This chapter is a warning bell—not to create fear, but to give awareness and wisdom. Some dangers are tempting, appearing harmless at first. But once you step in, it's hard to escape.

Some risks in life should be approached with wisdom and caution, while others should be avoided completely, like the plague. This chapter will help you identify what to stay away from before it's too late.

1. The Obvious Dangers – Avoid at All Costs

Some mistakes leave scars—some emotional, some financial, and some irreversible. These are the ones you should never experiment with.

Drugs, Alcoholism, and Substance Abuse

Many people flirt with drugs and alcohol, thinking they can control it. But addiction is a trap—once inside, escaping is painful. Drugs ruin careers, destroy families, and often end in financial, legal, or health disasters.

Example: Countless celebrities, athletes, and young professionals have lost everything due to substance abuse. Some died at the peak of success, proving that addiction does not care who you are.

Crime and Quick Money Schemes

Whether it's fraud, theft, or illegal dealings, many fall into the trap of "easy money." What seems like a shortcut to wealth often leads to prison, financial ruin, or worse.

Example: The world is filled with stories of successful people who lost everything because they tried to cheat the system. Even minor dishonesty can grow into a career-ending scandal.

Toxic Relationships and Manipulative People

Some people will drain your energy, self-worth, and confidence. Whether it's an abusive relationship, a jealous friend, or a manipulative boss—staying too long in toxic relationships can destroy you.

Lesson:

Learn to spot toxic people early and walk away without hesitation.

2. The Hidden Dangers – Approach with Extreme Wisdom

Some dangers are not obvious—they seem harmless at first but slowly consume your time, energy, and potential.

Social Media Overuse and Digital Addiction

The world is addicted to screens. Social media and gaming are designed to trap attention, control behavior, and waste time.

Comparison culture creates low self-esteem.
Endless scrolling destroys focus.
Video game addiction steals real-world opportunities.

Solution:

Control technology before it controls you. Set limits and choose real-life experiences over virtual distractions.

Wasting Time with the Wrong People

The wrong crowd can pull you down faster than any bad habit. Spending time with negative, unambitious, or lazy people will kill your drive before you realize it.

Solution:

Surround yourself with people who inspire, challenge, and uplift you.

Financial Irresponsibility

Bad money habits lead to lifelong struggles. Many people spend recklessly, borrow carelessly, and save nothing, only to wake up in a financial crisis.

Solution:

Learn financial discipline early—spend wisely, invest smartly, and avoid debt traps.

3. The Traps That Feel Like Success

Some dangers don't look like problems. In fact, they disguise themselves as success but slowly consume happiness, peace, and purpose.

The Trap of Materialism

Success is often measured by cars, watches, luxury, and lifestyle, but none of it guarantees happiness. People who chase material wealth often find themselves empty and dissatisfied even after achieving it.

Lesson:

Invest in relationships, experiences, and impact, not just wealth.

The "Always Busy" Lifestyle

Many confuse being busy with being successful. Some people work 80-hour weeks, sacrificing family, health, and friendships, only to realize they never truly lived.

Lesson: Success is about balance—work hard, but never at the cost of your well-being and relationships.

4. The Most Dangerous Mindset: "It Won't Happen to Me"

The biggest mistake people make is thinking "I can handle it" or "That won't happen to me."

No one plans to get addicted, but many do.

No one plans to go broke, but reckless spending leads there.

No one plans to ruin their life, but ignoring warnings leads to disaster.

Lesson:

Learn from other people's mistakes. Avoid what destroys, embrace what builds.

Practical Steps & Actionable Tips

1. Make decisions with the future in mind – Always ask, "How will this choice affect me in 5 years?"

1. Have a strong "No" mindset – If something feels dangerous or wrong, walk away instantly.

3. Choose friends wisely – Your circle determines your direction. Surround yourself with disciplined, motivated, and honest people.

4. Control your impulses – Just because something feels good now doesn't mean it's right.

5. Create personal "Non-Negotiables" – Set clear rules for what you will never do, no matter what.

Reflection Questions for the Reader

Am I flirting with anything dangerous, thinking I can handle it?

Who in my life is influencing me negatively?

Have I fallen into any hidden traps that are wasting my potential?

What is one bad habit or distraction I need to eliminate today?

Final Thought

This chapter is not about fear—it's about wisdom. The world is full of opportunities, but also traps that will destroy your future if you're not careful.

Some risks can be navigated with wisdom, but others must be avoided completely. Some fires are too dangerous to play with—don't even go near them.

Be smart. Be cautious. Be aware. Success is not just about what you do—it's also about what you avoid.

Choose wisely.

XVI

Biases, Social Evils, and the Drug Epidemic – The Hidden Chains of Society

"The world will not be destroyed by those who do evil, but by those who watch them without doing anything." – Albert Einstein

Why This Chapter Matters

We live in the most advanced age in human history, yet society still suffers from deep-rooted biases, social evils, and destructive habits.

Technology has connected the world, but it has also exposed its darkest sides—prejudice, addiction, crime, and moral decay. While we celebrate progress, we cannot ignore the social evils that continue to destroy lives, families, and entire communities.

Some of these problems are legacy issues—deeply ingrained in culture and history. Others are modern—born out of the digital age and the rapid changes in lifestyle. But whether old or new, they hold people back, steal potential, and damage societies.

This chapter is about awareness and action—understanding these issues and knowing how to rise above them.

1. The Invisible Chains: Biases That Still Hold Society Back

Bias is a silent social evil. It is not always obvious, but it controls thoughts, decisions, and opportunities. Many people live limited lives because of biases they never even question.

Common Biases That Destroy Fairness and Equality

Gender Bias

Women and men are still treated unequally in many parts of the world, limiting careers, education, and rights.

Example: Many industries still pay women less than men for the same job.

Racial and Ethnic Bias

Discrimination based on race or ethnicity creates barriers to success. Even today, people face unfair treatment just because of their background.

Lesson:

Intelligence, character, and capability are not limited by race or skin color.

Social Class Bias

The rich get richer while the poor struggle to break free from economic limits placed on them.

Lesson:

True success should be based on effort and ability, not privilege.

Age Bias

Younger people are often not taken seriously, while older people are pushed aside as outdated. ? Solution: Wisdom comes from experience, not just age. Respect both youth and maturity.

Final Thought:

Bias is a mental prison. The only way to break free is to question everything and judge people by their actions, not by labels.

2. The Digital Age and Modern Social Evils

Technology was supposed to improve society, but it has also created new dangers.

How Modern Technology Is Creating New Social Evils

The Rise of Fake News and Misinformation

The internet is full of lies, manipulated facts, and propaganda that divide people and spread hate.

Example: Many people believe fake stories on social media without checking facts, leading to riots, fear, and division.

Solution:

Verify everything before sharing. Be a seeker of truth, not a spreader of lies.

Cyberbullying and Online Hate

The anonymity of the internet has made bullying easier. Words destroy lives, leading to depression and even suicides.

Lesson:

If you wouldn't say it face-to-face, don't say it online.

Social Media Addiction and Mental Health Crises

People compare themselves to fake perfection on Instagram and TikTok, leading to self-doubt and anxiety.

Lesson:

Social media is a highlight reel, not reality. Don't let it control your self-worth.

3. The Drug Epidemic – A Crisis That Destroys Generations

One of the deadliest modern social evils is the drug epidemic. Addiction is destroying young lives, families, and entire communities.

Why Do People Fall Into the Drug Trap?

Curiosity and Peer Pressure – Many try it "just once," but once is all it takes to get hooked.

Stress and Escapism – People use drugs to escape problems, but drugs create bigger problems.

Glorification in Media – Movies, music, and celebrities make drug use look "cool" when in reality, it leads to destruction.

Example: Countless celebrities have died young because of drug overdose. Their talent and success couldn't save them from addiction.

Lesson:

Never even try it. Drugs are a fire that burns lives and futures.

The Deadly Impact of Drugs

Destroys careers – Addicts lose focus, jobs, and ambition.

Ruins families – Addiction hurts parents, children, and relationships.

Leads to crime – Many resort to theft and violence to support their habit.

Can kill in one mistake – One overdose, one bad pill, and it's game over.

Final Thought:

Drug dealers don't sell happiness—they sell death in disguise.

4. How to Rise Above These Social Evils

The world is not perfect, but you have the power to choose a different path.

- Educate Yourself – Awareness is the first step to change. Question biases, challenge social evils, and seek truth.

- Surround Yourself with Strong-Minded People – Choose friends who push you toward success, not destruction.
- Use Technology Wisely – Instead of wasting time on distractions, use digital tools for learning, growth, and opportunities.

- Speak Up Against Injustice – Silence allows social evils to grow. Use your voice for good.

- Stay Away from Dangerous Lifestyles – If something feels wrong, it probably is. Walk away.

- Be the Example – The best way to change the world is to be a person of integrity and inspire others to do the same.

Reflection Questions for the Reader

Do I challenge biases, or do I follow them blindly?

Am I using technology wisely, or is it using me?

Have I ever shared or believed fake news without verifying?

Am I making choices that protect me from destructive habits?

What can I do to be part of the solution instead of the problem?

Final Thought

We live in a time of incredible opportunity, but also great danger. Biases, social evils, and addictions are designed to control and destroy lives.

The key to success in today's world is awareness, discipline, and courage—the courage to challenge what is wrong, to avoid what is destructive, and to build a life that is meaningful and ethical.

Break free from mental prisons, dangerous traps, and social lies. Choose a path of wisdom, awareness, and positive impact.

The future belongs to those who can rise above the distractions and evils of the world.

Will you be one of them?

XVII

You Always Have Help – The Path Back is Always Open

"No matter how far you've gone in the wrong direction, you can always turn around." –
Anonymous

Why This Chapter Matters

Life is unpredictable. Some people make mistakes that seem too big to fix. Others feel too lost, too broken, or too guilty to return to the right path. But here's the truth: No one is beyond redemption. No one is too far gone to come back.

The world may judge and reject, but help is always available—through family, faith, and the institutions of law and welfare. Even in the darkest moments, there is a way back to forgiveness, restoration, and a fresh start.

This chapter is about hope, second chances, and the promise that you are never alone. No matter how lost you feel, you can return.

The Lost Sheep: A Story of Unwavering Love

One of the most beautiful parables in the Bible is the story of the lost sheep (Luke 15:3-7).

A shepherd had 100 sheep, but when one got lost, he left the 99 to find the one that was missing. He did not say, "I have 99, so it doesn't matter." Instead, he searched until he found the lost one. And when he did, he celebrated, not scolded the sheep for wandering off.

Lesson:

No matter how far you've strayed, you are valuable. Even if the world forgets you, God never does. There is always a way back, and there is always joy in your return.

The Prodigal Son: The Power of Forgiveness and Returning

Another powerful story is the Prodigal Son (Luke 15:11-32).

A young man demanded his inheritance early and wasted it on reckless living. Soon, he was broke, starving, and ashamed. He thought, "I am not worthy to go back home." But eventually, he decided to return to his father, even if it meant being treated as a servant.

Instead of anger or punishment, his father ran to him, hugged him, and threw a feast to celebrate his return.

Lesson:

There may be consequences for bad choices, but forgiveness is always available. No matter what you've done, you can always come home.

The Reality of Coming Back – Consequences and Redemption

Yes, there may be losses to pay for mistakes. The prodigal son lost his wealth and time. A person who falls into addiction, crime, or toxic habits may face damaged relationships, financial ruin, or lost years.

But coming back is still worth it.

Returning means:

- Accepting responsibility for mistakes.
- Learning from the past instead of being trapped by guilt.
- Rebuilding trust, step by step.
- Choosing restoration over regret.

Truth:

The longer you stay away, the harder it becomes. Don't wait. Start now.

Where to Find Help When You Feel Lost

Many people don't return because they don't know where to turn. But help is always available.

1. **Family** – The First Support System

- Your family may not be perfect, but they are the ones who truly care.
- They may be disappointed in your mistakes, but most families would rather have you back than see you destroyed.
- Even if you feel ashamed, pick up the phone, visit home, or ask for forgiveness.

Example:

Many former addicts, criminals, or lost souls found healing when they reconciled with their family.

2. Faith – A Source of Strength and Guidance

- God's mercy is bigger than your mistakes.
- Faith communities offer guidance, counseling, and support for those seeking a new path.
- Prayer, meditation, and reflection help clear guilt and find purpose again.

Example:

Countless people have turned their lives around through faith, finding peace, purpose, and a second chance.

3. Institutions of Law and Welfare – A Path to Restoration

- Legal help exists for those who want to change but feel trapped by past mistakes. ✓ Rehabilitation programs, support groups, and counseling services provide a structured way to recover.
- Welfare and community programs help those in financial, emotional, or mental crisis.

Example:

Many people who committed crimes served their sentence, rebuilt their reputation, and now help others avoid the same mistakes.

Taking the First Step – How to Return When You Feel Lost

Returning is hard because of fear, shame, and doubt. But every comeback story starts with one decision.

Step 1: Admit You Want to Change

- Stop making excuses.
- Acknowledge your mistakes but don't let them define you.
- Be willing to start fresh.

Step 2: Seek Help and Guidance

- Talk to someone you trust—a parent, sibling, friend, mentor, or faith leader.
- Join a support group or rehabilitation program if needed.
- Remove yourself from negative environments that pull you back into bad habits.

Step 3: Take Small, Consistent Steps

- Start with one honest conversation—say "I need help."
- Make one daily commitment—stay sober, be accountable, or take a positive action.
- Accept that trust takes time—people may doubt you at first, but stay consistent.

Example:

Someone who broke trust in a relationship doesn't earn it back overnight—but over months or years of changed behavior, trust can be restored.

What Happens When You Return?

You Rebuild Your Life – Every comeback story starts with a choice. Your past does not define your future.

You Inspire Others – Your story can help someone else who is struggling.

You Experience Real Freedom – Guilt, shame, and fear fade when you take responsibility and make things right.

Truth:

The world won't always welcome you back—but the right people will. Focus on those who believe in you.

Reflection Questions for the Reader

Is there a part of my life where I need to return and make things right?

Have I been avoiding help because of pride or fear?

Who can I reach out to today for support?

Do I believe I am worthy of a second chance? (Hint: You are.)

Final Thought

You are never too far gone to come back. Mistakes happen, but redemption is real.

The lost sheep was found. The prodigal son was embraced. And you, too, can return to the people, purpose, and future you were meant for.

- No matter what you've done, you can choose a better path.
- No matter how far you've wandered, you can return home.
- No matter how broken you feel, help is always available.

Your past does not define you. Your choices today do.
Come back. The door is open.

XVIII

Final Words: The Journey Ahead – Your Life, Your Choices

"Every moment is a fresh beginning." – T.S. Eliot

Why This Matters

You've read through pages of wisdom, experiences, and warnings. You've seen the power of discipline, the weight of responsibility, the urgency of resilience, and the beauty of second chances. But now comes the most important part—what will you do with it?

This is not just another book. This is your roadmap—a navigation guide for life that shows you the paths, pitfalls, and principles that will shape your future. But reading alone does nothing. Action is what changes lives.

This final chapter is a challenge, a wake-up call, and a reminder—that your story is still being written, and you hold the pen.

So, let's end strong. Let's break it down. Let's make it compelling, fun, edgy, and fulfilling—because your life deserves nothing less.

1. *Your Life is a One-Way Trip – Make It Count*

Imagine life as a one-way ticket on a high-speed train. You can't go back. You can't stop time. You can only move forward.

Some people waste their journey staring at the scenery—passive, waiting for something to happen.

Others complain about the train—upset about the speed, the people, or the destination.

But the winners? They make every stop count. They learn, grow, and take action at every opportunity.

Reality Check:

You don't get to rewind time. You only get one shot at this. So, will you waste it, or will you make it count?

- Build something meaningful.
- Chase what truly matters.
- Avoid the distractions and nonsense.
- Leave behind something worth remembering.

This isn't just motivation. This is real life. And if you don't take control of your choices, someone else will do it for you.

2. The Secret to an Epic Life – Own Your Story

Most people live life like passengers, waiting for something to happen. But here's the truth:
No one is coming to save you.

- No magical opportunity will knock on your door.
- No one will hand you success.
- No one owes you anything.

If you want something, you have to take it, build it, and fight for it.

Example:

Every legend—from athletes to business icons—had to take control. They didn't wait. They acted.

- Michael Jordan didn't wait for approval—he outworked everyone.
- Elon Musk didn't wait for permission—he created industries.
- Oprah Winfrey didn't wait for an easy road—she paved her own.

If you don't own your story, someone else will write it for you. And trust me, you won't like their version.

1.

The Pitfalls That Will Try to Derail You

You've learned about discipline, responsibility, resilience, and avoiding dangers. But the truth? Life will throw obstacles at you.

Watch out for these silent killers:

Excuses – The easiest way to fail is to blame everything but yourself.

Laziness – If you don't push yourself, no one else will.

Toxic People – Surround yourself with winners, not energy vampires.

Fear – Fear is the enemy of success. Do it scared, but do it anyway.

Solution:

Recognize these traps early. Cut them out like a disease. Choose progress over comfort.

4.

The Difference Between Success and Failure? One Simple Thing.

What separates the winners from the losers?
Not intelligence.
Not talent.
Not luck.
The answer - **CONSISTENCY**.

- The best athletes train every single day—not just when they feel like it.
- The best entrepreneurs keep building even when no one believes in them.

- The best relationships are nurtured daily, not just when convenient.

Lesson:

Small actions, done consistently, create huge results over time.

Want to get fit?
Do 30 minutes of exercise every day.
Want to master a skill?
Practice for 1 hour daily, no excuses.
Want to be successful?
Show up, do the work, repeat.
The formula is simple, but most people fail because they lack the patience to stay consistent.

5. The Only Competition That Matters? The Person in the Mirror.

Forget comparing yourself to others. Your real competition is YOU.

- Are you better today than you were yesterday?
- Are you making progress or just making excuses?
- Are you moving forward or stuck in the same cycle?

Reality Check:

No one else's success takes away from yours. Focus on becoming the best version of yourself.

6.

The Three Questions That Will Change Your Life

At the end of every day, ask yourself:
What did I do today that made me better?
What am I wasting my time on?
If I continue this path, where will I be in five years?
These three questions will force you to take responsibility and ensure you don't drift through life.

7.

The Last Chapter is Unwritten – You Decide How It Ends

This book doesn't end with this chapter—because your story is still being written.
You've read the lessons.
You've seen the examples.
You've been given the roadmap.
Now, what will you do with it?

- Will you take action, or will you close this book and go back to old habits?
- Will you make your life extraordinary, or will you let distractions win?
- Will you choose growth, purpose, and impact, or will you waste your time on meaningless things?

The choice is yours.

Truth:

You don't get a second shot at life. Make this one count.

Final Thought

The Future is Yours to Create

No one else is responsible for your happiness, success, or impact.

You define your future.

You control your choices.

You write the final chapter.

So take this knowledge.

Use it.

Apply it.

And build a life that is legendary.

Because when your time is up, you want to look back with pride, not regret.

This is your moment.

Go make it happen.

Lets Now Begin !

Don't just close this book. Take one action today—no matter how small—that moves you forward.

Your future starts NOW. ?

www.ingramcontent.com/pod-product-compliance
Lightning Source LLC
Chambersburg PA
CBHW031304130726
47988CB00007B/2716